LINDSEY
THE GIS PROFESSIONAL

A GIS Mapping Story

by Tyler Danielson, GIS Specialist
Illustrated by Lime Valley Advertising, Inc.

©2020 Bolton & Menk, Inc.

BOLTON & MENK

Real People. Real Solutions.

Esri Press
REDLANDS | CALIFORNIA

Hey there! My name is Lindsey and I'm a GIS Professional.

GIS stands for Geographic Information Systems, which means I make maps and analyze **spatial data**.

The first thing you need to make a map is **data**. Data is information and facts about a specific thing or place in our world. Data is 'spatial' when it has a location, like an address for a house.

Spatial data can come in two forms. Vector data is made of points, lines, and polygons. Raster data is a grid of data where each cell is a pixel—this is usually a picture.

Maps also include **non-spatial data** like the species of a tree or the style of a fence. This data is recorded in a table and is connected to its location.

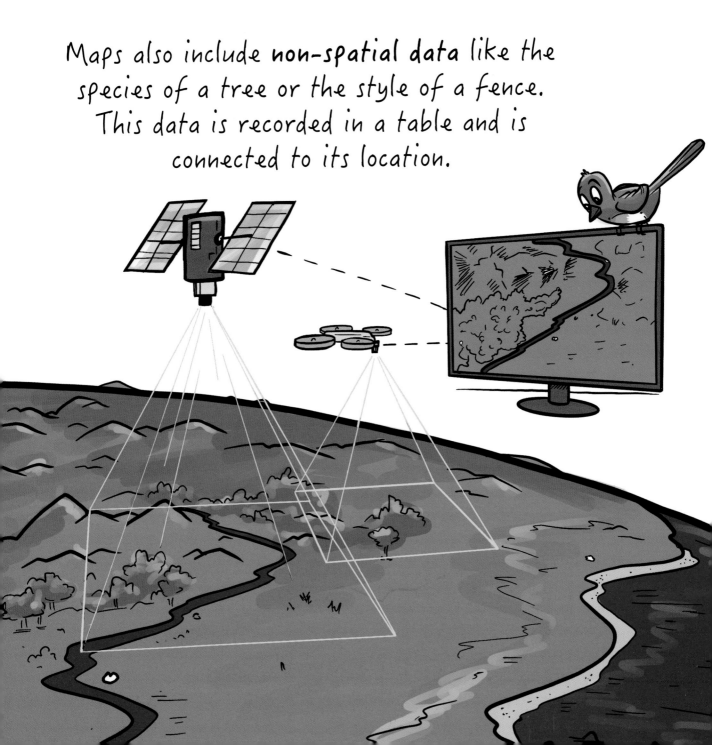

Let's go collect some data with a smartphone at my favorite park.

A smartphone uses satellites in space that send a signal back to Earth to figure out where the phone is.

Some data is collected as a polygon,
like this lake. We can use the smartphone
to record the boundary of the lake.

We also need to map this fence.
We can collect it as a line.

Let's walk along the fence and record its location.

Finally, let's collect the location of this tree as a point because it is in one spot. We can also record that this tree is a maple tree and measure just how tall and big around it is.

The extra data (non-spatial data) collected on the tree is called attributes. These attributes tell us extra information about each location we recorded.

Now, to finish my map let's have some fun and fly my drone WAAAAY up in the sky and take a picture of the ground.

This picture is **raster data.** We can use this picture as the first layer of our map, called a basemap.

Now that we have all the data, let's make a map!

I'll add the picture of the park and the other data we collected. See how the points, lines, and polygons match the features in the picture?

Now let's add a **north arrow** to show direction and a **scale bar** to show how far things in real life are on the map.

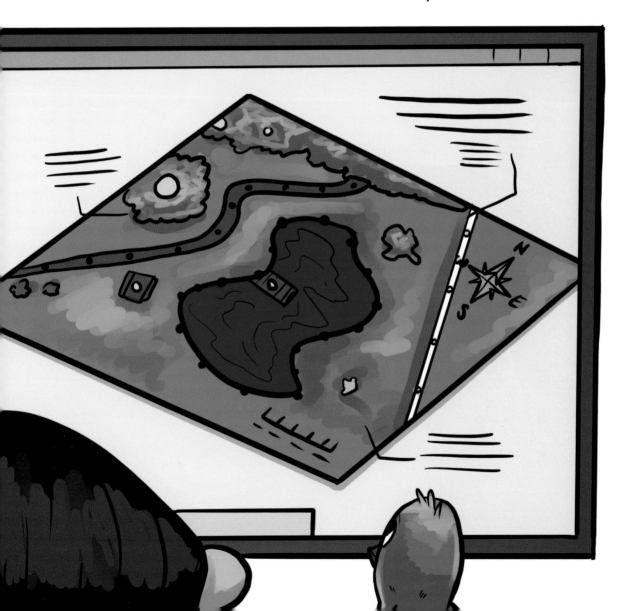

We will need to do some **analysis** of the data before we share this with our engineers. Then they will know where they can build and where they can't.

Great job! You made your first map!

Glossary

Analysis — The process of taking something complex and reviewing it in smaller parts to gain a better understanding.

Data — Information and facts about a specific thing or place in our world.

North Arrow — A map element that shows which way is north.

Non-spatial Data — The attributes of a feature, like the species of a tree or the number of people living in a city (population).

Raster Data — Many dots organized into a grid where each cell contains a value.

(Examples: temperature, aerial photos, and elevation)

Scale Bar — A map element that shows how far something is in real life on the map.

(Example: 1 inch on the map equals 5 miles in real life)

Spatial Data — Data that has a location, like an address or longitude and latitude coordinates.

Vector Data — A collection of points, lines, and polygons representing things or places on a map.

(Examples: Points = trees or signs, Lines = roads or rivers, Polygons = lakes or a building)

Coming soon!

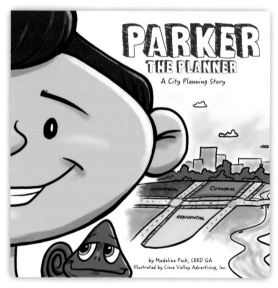

Learn more at LindseyLovesMaps.com.